COMETS

AND MORE SPACE SPEEDSTERS

An imprint of Abdo Publishing
abdobooks.com

ANN WILLIAMS

TAKE IT TO THE XTREME!

GET READY FOR AN EXTREME ADVENTURE! THE PAGES OF THIS BOOK WILL TAKE YOU INTO THE THRILLING WORLD OF ASTRONOMICAL WONDERS. WHEN YOU HAVE FINISHED READING THIS BOOK, TAKE THE XTREME CHALLENGE ON PAGE 45 ABOUT WHAT YOU'VE LEARNED!

ABDOBOOKS.COM
Published by Abdo Publishing, a division of ABDO, PO Box 398166, Minneapolis, Minnesota 55439.

Printed in the United States of America, North Mankato, MN.
102024
012025

Design: Kelly Doudna, Mighty Media, Inc.
Production: Mighty Media, Inc.
Editor: Katherine Chu

Cover Photograph: ESA & NASA
Interior Photographs: Alessandro Bianconi/Edu INAF/Flickr, pp. 6-7; Dai Jianfeng/IAU OAE, pp. 32-33; Doug West/Wikimedia Commons, pp. 8-9; E. Kolmhofer, H. Raab; Johannes-Kepler-Observatory, Linz, Austria/Wikimedia Commons, pp. 4-5; ESA/ATG medialab, pp. 26-27; ESA & NASA, p. 1; ESO/E. Slawik/Wikimedia Commons, pp. 18-19; Greg Willis/Wikimedia Commons, pp. 12-13; Melle Le Jeuneux/Wikimedia Commons, p. 17; Michael Karrer/Flickr, p. 44; Myrabella/Wikimedia Commons, pp. 14-15; NASA/Eric James, pp. 24-25; NASA, ESA, and D. Jewitt (UCLA), pp. 10-11; NASA/Johns Hopkins APL/Steve Gribben, pp. 36-37, 42-43; NASA/JPL-Caltech, pp. 30-31, 38-39; NASA/JPLCaltech/LMSS, pp. 22-23; NASA/JPL/MPS/DLR/IDA/Björn Jónsson/Wikimedia Commons, pp. 28-29; NASA TV, pp. 40-41; NASA/Wikimedia Commons, pp. 20-21; NASA/W. Liller/Wikimedia Commons, pp. 16-17; USGS, pp. 34-35
Design Elements: Arafat/Adobe Stock (header background); pixel/Adobe Stock (universe); Sergey Nivens/Shutterstock Images (header background)

LIBRARY OF CONGRESS CONTROL NUMBER: 2024938308
PUBLISHER'S CATALOGING-IN-PUBLICATION DATA
Names: Williams, Ann, author.
Title: Comets and more space speedsters / by Ann Williams
Description: Minneapolis, Minnesota : ABDO Publishing, 2025 | Series: Xtreme universe | Includes online resources and index.
Identifiers: ISBN 9781098295042 (lib. bdg.) | ISBN 9798384915096 (ebook)
Subjects: LCSH: Comets--Juvenile literature. | Meteors--Juvenile literature. | Falling stars--Juvenile literature. | Universe--Juvenile literature. | Outer space--Exploration--Juvenile literature. | Astronomy—Juvenile literature.
Classification: DDC 523.112--dc23

CONTENTS

CHAPTER 1

STARGAZING AT NIGHT

You are on a camping trip with your family. It's a clear night, so you set up your telescope to look at the sky. Suddenly, you see a moving bright spot with a fuzzy tail. It's a comet!

From Earth, comets don't seem to move very fast. But they can go more than 100,000 miles per hour (161,000 kmh). Comets are some of the fastest objects in the universe!

Comets have two tails. One tail is white and made of dust. The second is bluish and made of ions.

CHAPTER 2

WHAT IS A COMET?

Comets are balls of ice and dust. They orbit the sun in large circles that take them to the **outer** edges of the solar system. As a comet moves closer to the sun, the ice starts turning into a gas called **plasma**. The plasma mixes with dust, forming a long **streak** behind the comet. This streak is called a tail.

The ball of a comet is called the nucleus. The nucleus of most comets is about 6 miles (10 km) across. A comet's tail can be millions of miles long!

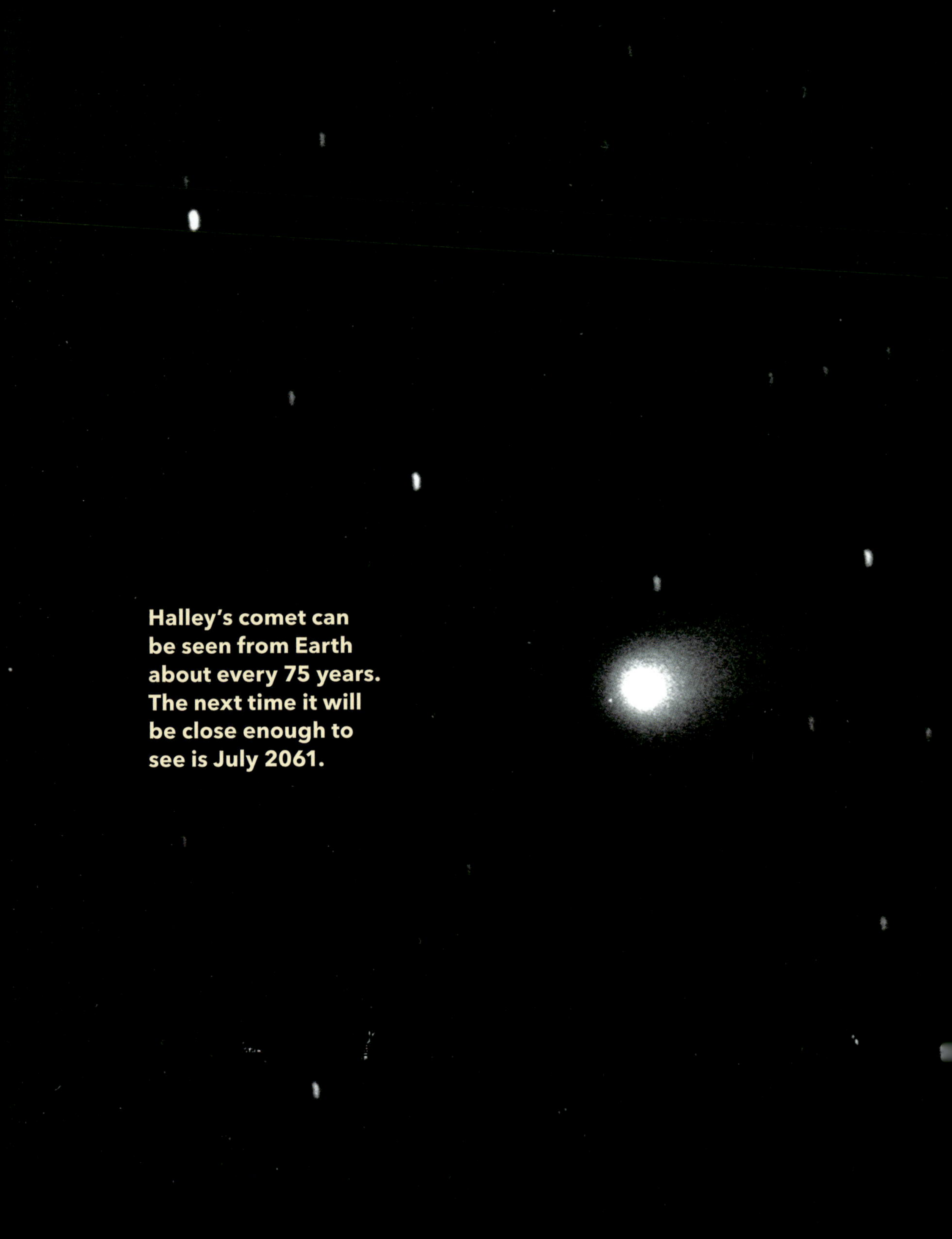

Halley's comet can be seen from Earth about every 75 years. The next time it will be close enough to see is July 2061.

There are many comets in space. Among the most famous is Halley's comet. It was named after English astronomer Edmond Halley. In the 1700s, Halley discovered that comets orbit the sun. He **predicted** when Halley's comet would be visible from Earth again.

Comet Hale-Bopp is another well-known comet. It has a very long orbit. It takes 2,534 years for Hale-Bopp to orbit the sun once!

Not all comets orbit Earth's sun. In 2019, Comet Borisov was discovered. It is the first comet known to have come from outside the solar system. Instead of orbiting Earth's sun, it just passed through our solar system, never to return.

Borisov is one of the fastest comets. It moves at 110,000 miles per hour (177,000 kmh).

CHAPTER 3

COMET HISTORY

Historians believe Ancestral Puebloans in Chaco Canyon, New Mexico, created a three-symbol pictograph depicting a supernova in 1054 CE. Some astronomers think that the drawing next to the pictograph is of Halley's comet.

People have observed comets for thousands of years. Ancient people feared comets. They thought comets were bad **omens**. Chinese astronomers in the 1000s BCE **described** the comets in detail. They also listed **disasters** they believed each comet caused.

Greek philosopher Aristotle was one of the first to try to explain what caused comets and how they moved. He thought comets were created by air catching fire in Earth's atmosphere. This made people fear comets even more. They continued to blame comets for Earth's **disasters** until the 1500s CE.

The Bayeux Tapestry from the 1070s includes a scene of a group of men looking at Halley's comet.

In 1759, French astronomer Nicolas Louis de Lacaille (*inset*) named Halley's comet in honor of Edmond Halley.

In 1577, Danish astronomer Tycho Brahe discovered a way to measure how far away comets were. He realized they were outside of Earth's atmosphere.

Then, in 1682, Halley observed a comet similar to those **described** in 1531 and 1607. He believed it was the same comet. Halley correctly **predicted** it would appear again in 1758. But he died before he could see it.

CHAPTER 4

OBSERVING COMETS

Hale-Bopp flew by Earth in 1997. It was 1,000 times brighter than Halley's comet. It was even visible from light-polluted cities.

Some comets are visible without a telescope. They are easier to see outside of cities, where there is less **light pollution**.

Astronomers can track comets. They share when and where the comets will be visible.

Astronomers use special telescopes to discover and observe comets that are farther away. The National Aeronautics and Space Administration (**NASA**) **launched** the James Webb Space Telescope in 2021 to study space, including comets.

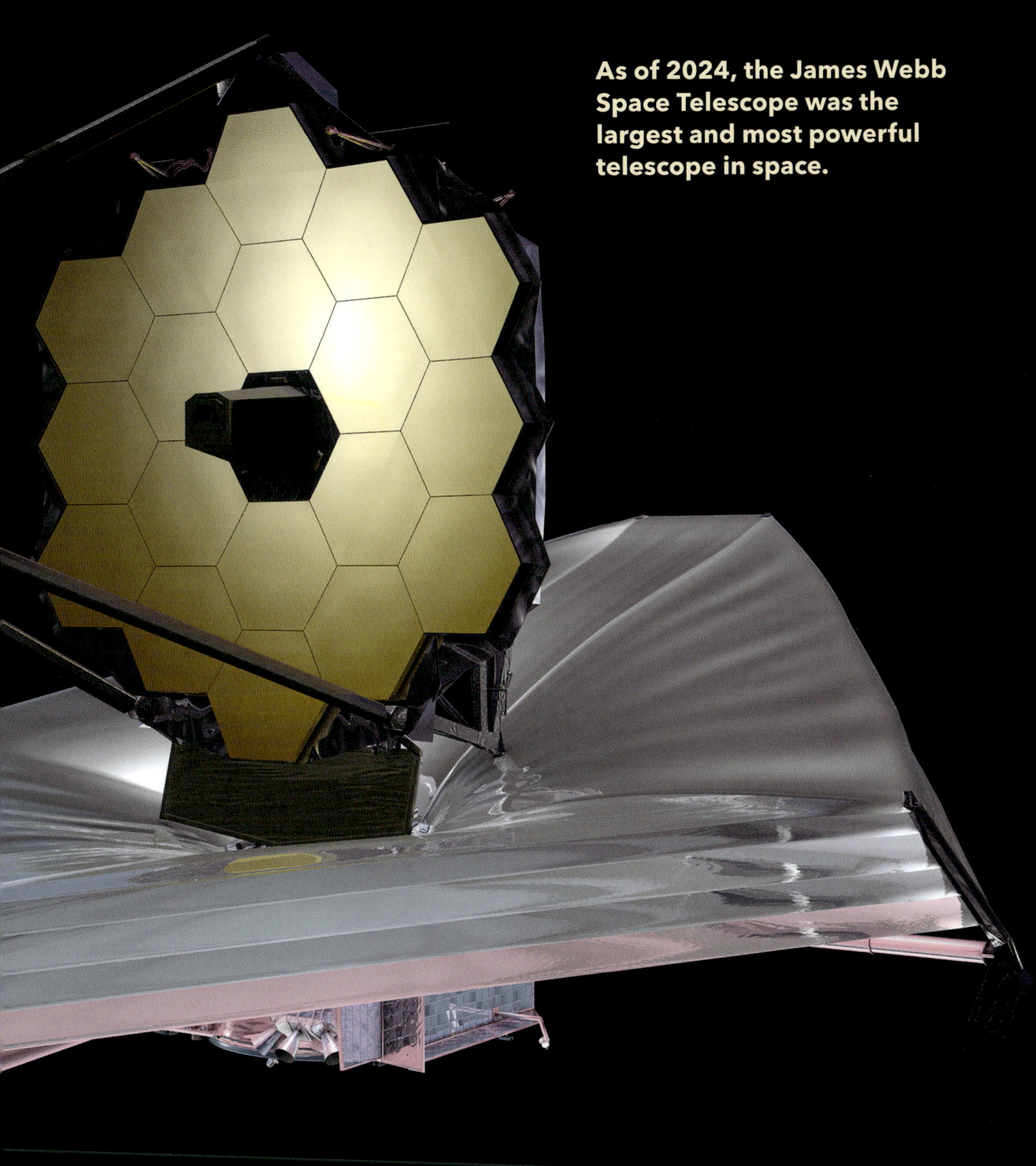

As of 2024, the James Webb Space Telescope was the largest and most powerful telescope in space.

CHAPTER 5

MODERN SCIENCE

Today's astronomers study comets using photos taken by the James Webb Space Telescope and Hubble Space Telescope. **NASA** also studies comets using spacecraft. These spacecraft take photos of comets. They also gather comet dust and **particle** samples.

XTREME FACT

Astronomers have identified more than 3,800 comets.

Launched in 1999, Stardust was the first NASA spacecraft mission to retrieve samples from a comet.

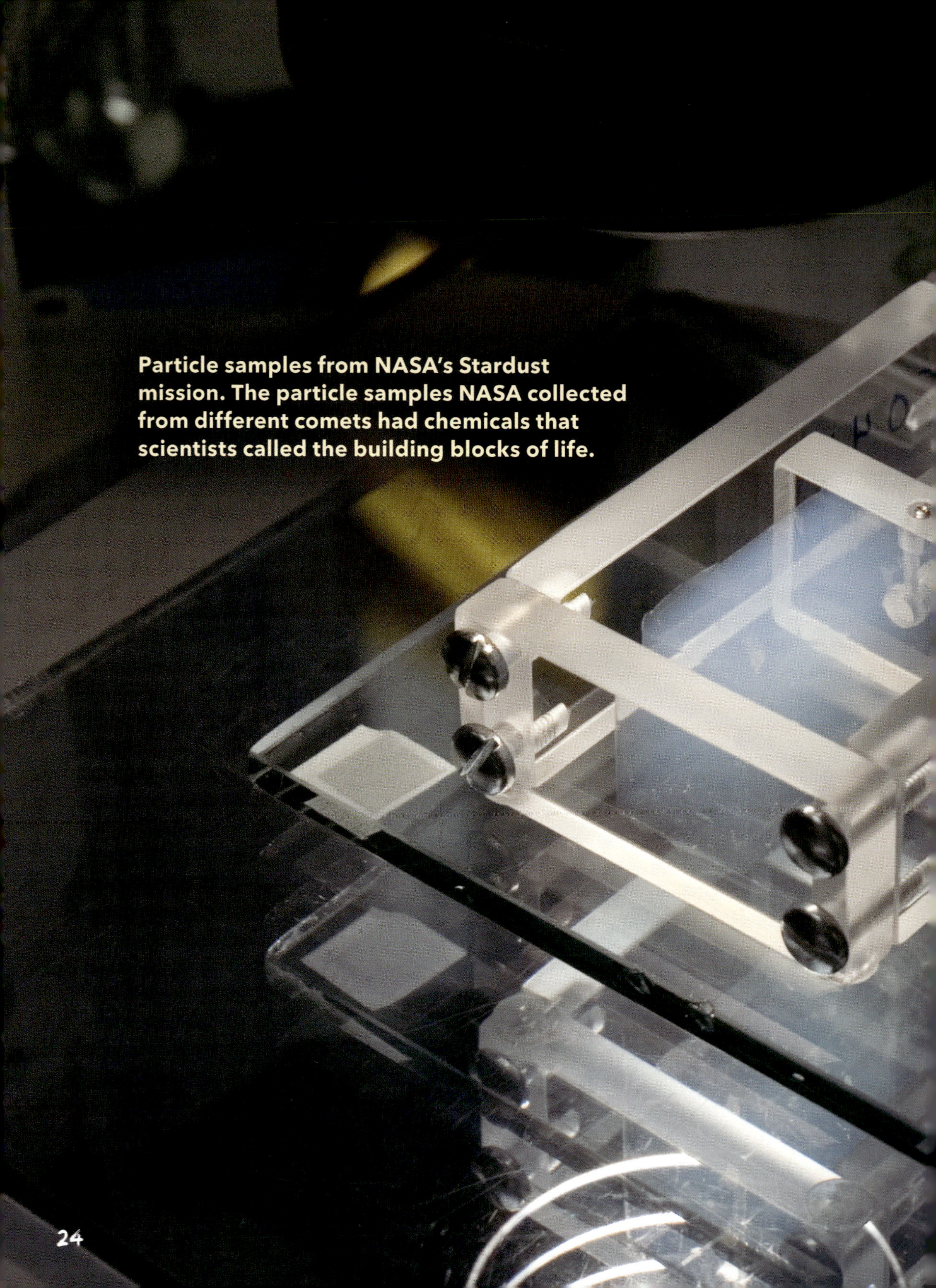

Particle samples from NASA's Stardust mission. The particle samples NASA collected from different comets had chemicals that scientists called the building blocks of life.

Astronomers believe the ice and dust in comets are left over from when the solar system formed 4.6 **billion** years ago. Many astronomers study comets to understand how the universe and solar system formed.

Some astronomers think comets may have brought water to Earth, helping life form. They hope that studying comets will help them learn how life could exist on other planets.

ASTEROIDS FLYING BY

The largest object in the asteroid belt is dwarf planet Ceres (*right*).

Comets are not the only objects whizzing around space. Asteroids are fast space objects that orbit the sun but stay closer to it than comets do. Most asteroids are in a ring called the asteroid belt. The asteroid belt orbits the sun and is located between Mars and Jupiter.

XTREME FACT

There are about 1.3 million asteroids in the solar system.

Asteroids are made of leftover rock from when the solar system formed. They range in size from less than 33 feet (10 m) to 329 miles (530 km) across. Asteroids move at about 38,000 to 55,000 miles per hour (61,000 to 88,000 kmh).

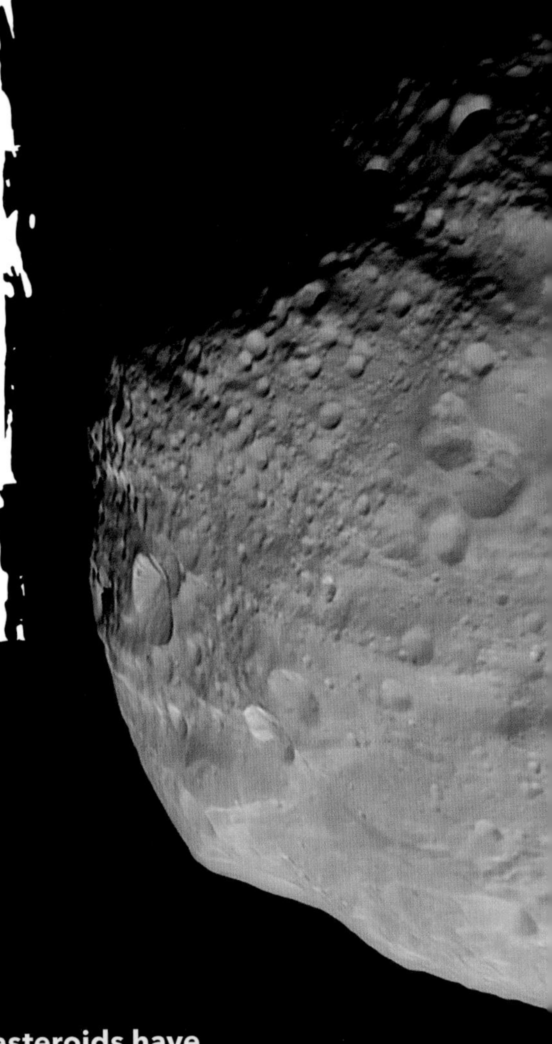

Some large asteroids have names. The biggest one in our solar system is named Vesta.

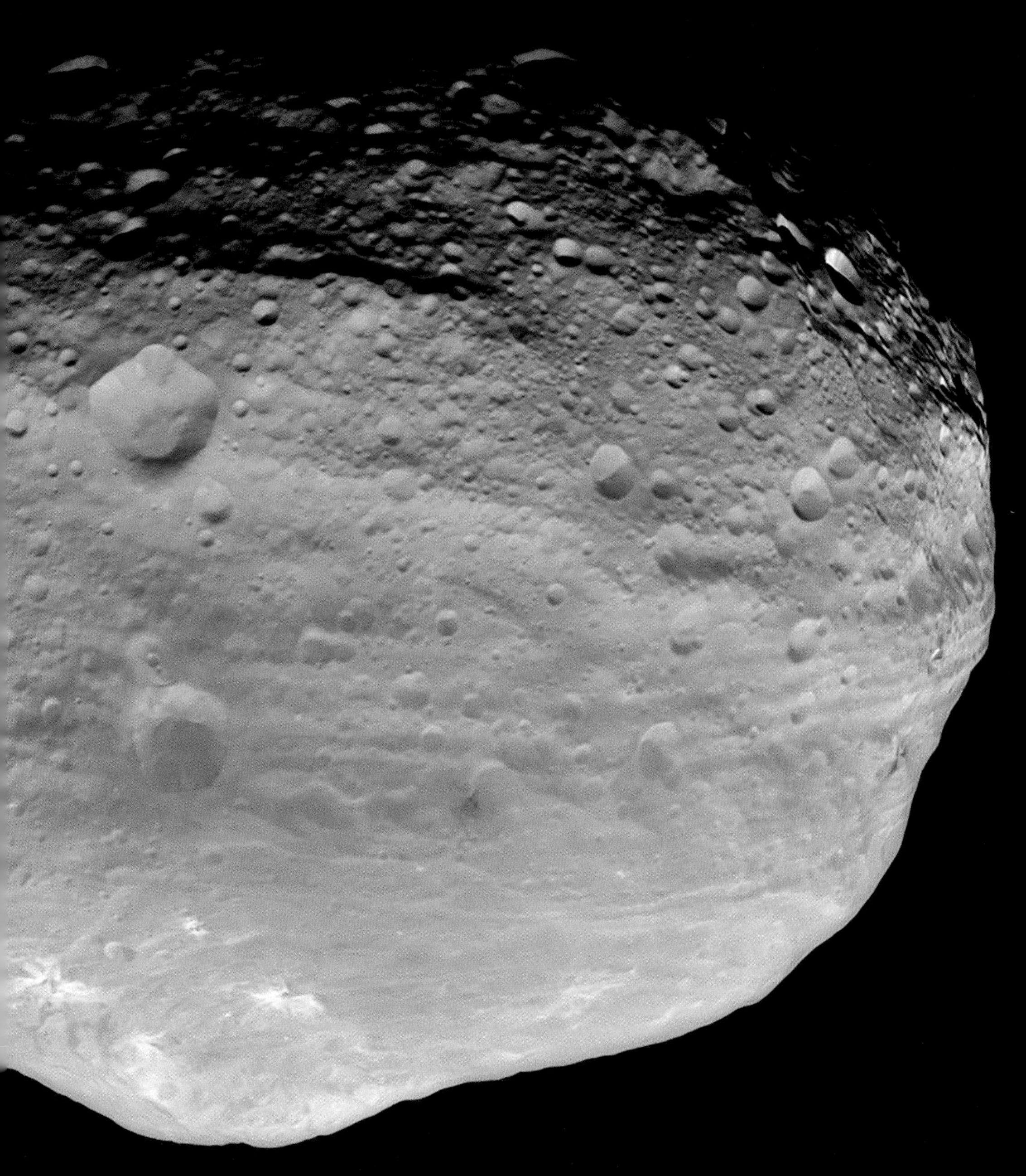

CHAPTER 7

MILLIONS OF METEOROIDS

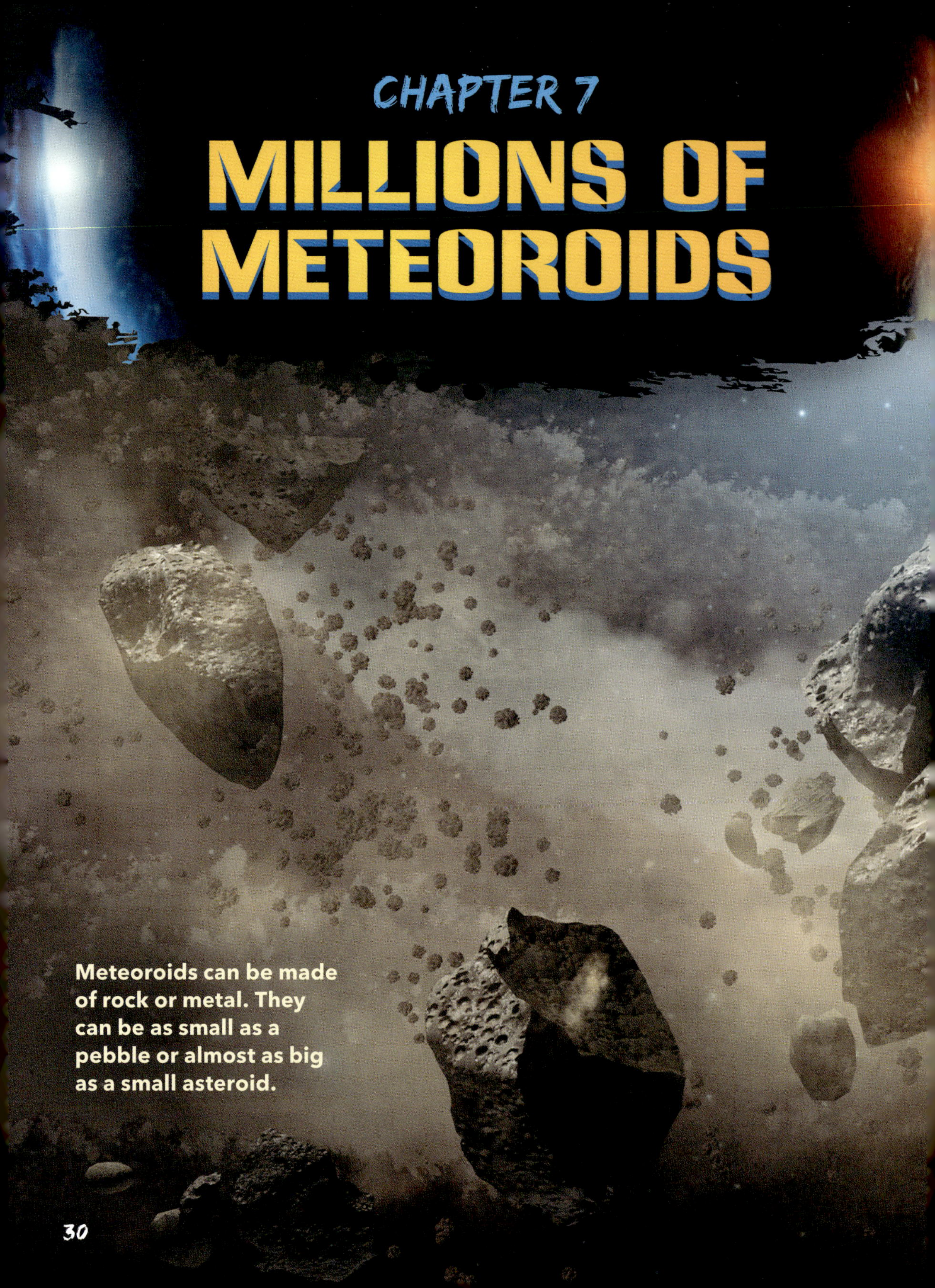

Meteoroids can be made of rock or metal. They can be as small as a pebble or almost as big as a small asteroid.

Other speedy space objects include meteoroids. Meteoroids are pieces that have broken off comets, asteroids, and planets. Meteoroids also orbit the sun. The fastest meteoroids can reach speeds of more than 90,000 miles per hour (145,000 kmh).

There are many millions of meteoroids in space. They often crash into other space objects. These include comets, planets, asteroids, and other meteoroids. Meteoroids that enter Earth's or another planet's atmosphere are called meteors. Most meteors burn up in Earth's atmosphere.

The Geminid meteor shower seen from China. When there are multiple meteors seen within a short period of time, it's called a meteor shower.

XTREME FACT

Have you heard of a falling star? This is a bright streak of light in the sky. But it isn't actually a star. It's a meteor burning up in Earth's atmosphere.

CHAPTER 8

METEORITE IMPACT!

A crater made by a meteorite in Arizona. Most meteorites don't do any harm. But some are big enough to damage buildings and make craters in the ground.

XTREME FACT

Many experts think that dinosaurs died out millions of years ago because of a comet or asteroid that struck Earth.

Sometimes, meteors are too large to burn up entirely in Earth's atmosphere. Meteors that land on Earth's surface are called meteorites. As many as 10,000 meteorites land on Earth each year.

Some scientists worry that one day a huge space object, such as an asteroid or comet, will crash into Earth. This could destroy large areas or even make life

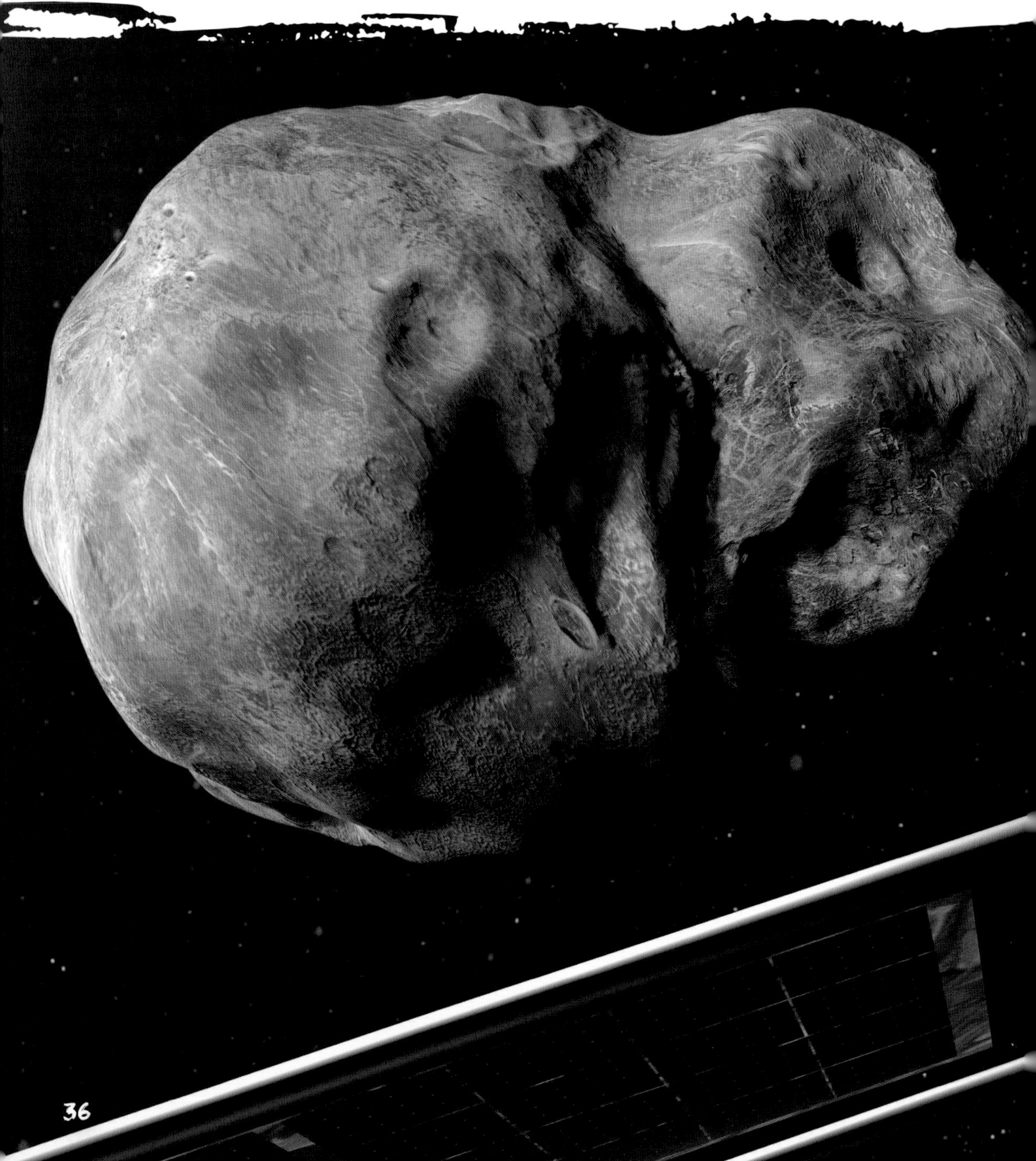

on Earth impossible. Scientists use space telescopes to watch for large objects heading toward Earth. They also try to find ways to stop a **collision**.

In 2022, NASA's DART spacecraft successfully crashed into the asteroid Dimorphos. The mission was a test to see if NASA could redirect an asteroid.

CHAPTER 9

ARTIFICIAL SPACE OBJECTS

In addition to naturally occurring objects, there are also fast artificial space objects. These include satellites. Most satellites stay within 1,200 miles (2,000 km) of Earth. They need to move quickly to avoid the pull of Earth's gravity. These satellites orbit Earth at 17,000 miles per hour (27,400 kmh).

Satellites help scientists study the clouds, oceans, land, and air on Earth. Some even explore space bodies such as planets, stars, asteroids, and more.

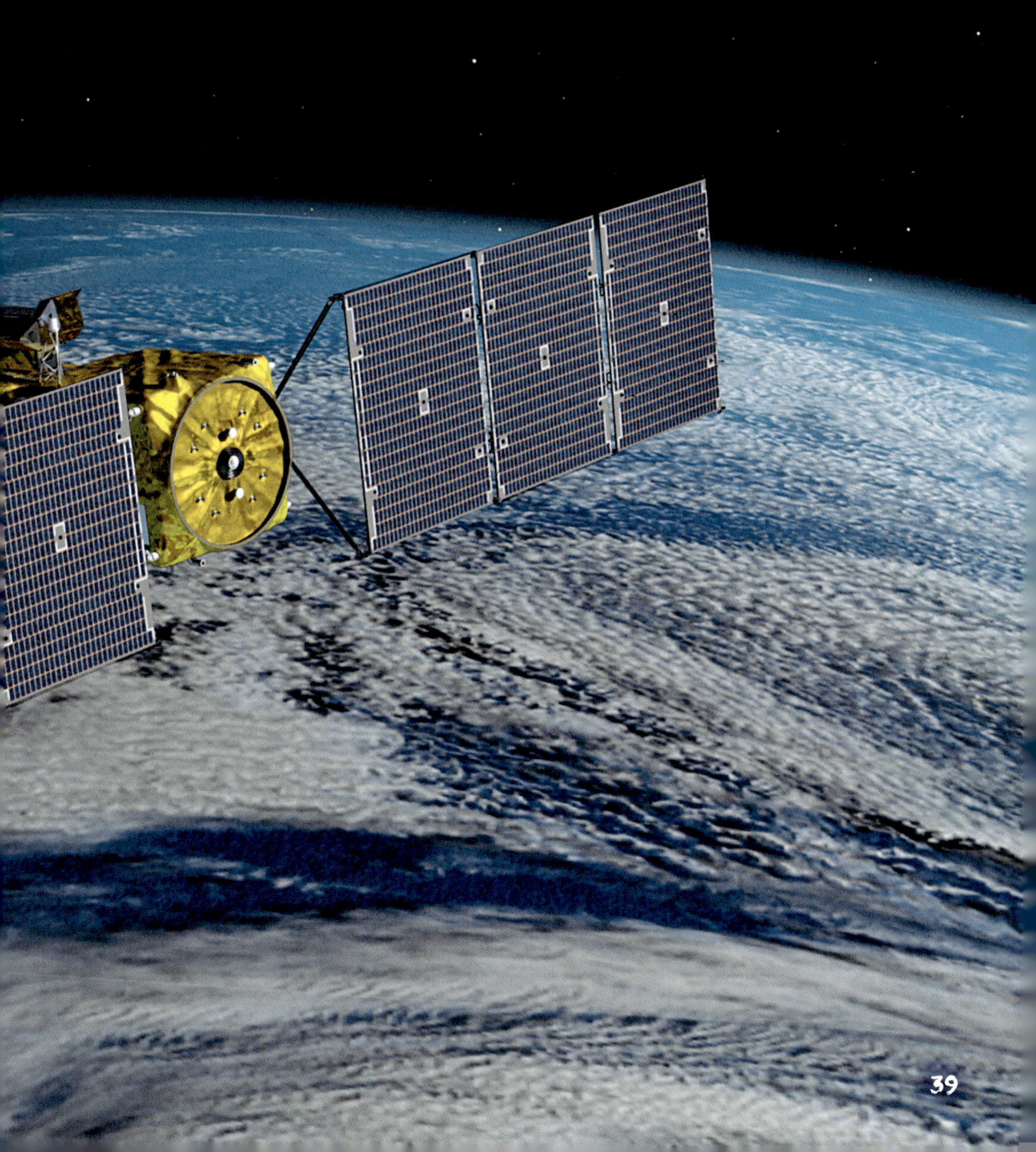

Space junk also includes human waste and a tool bag lost by astronauts while they were performing maintenance outside the International Space Station.

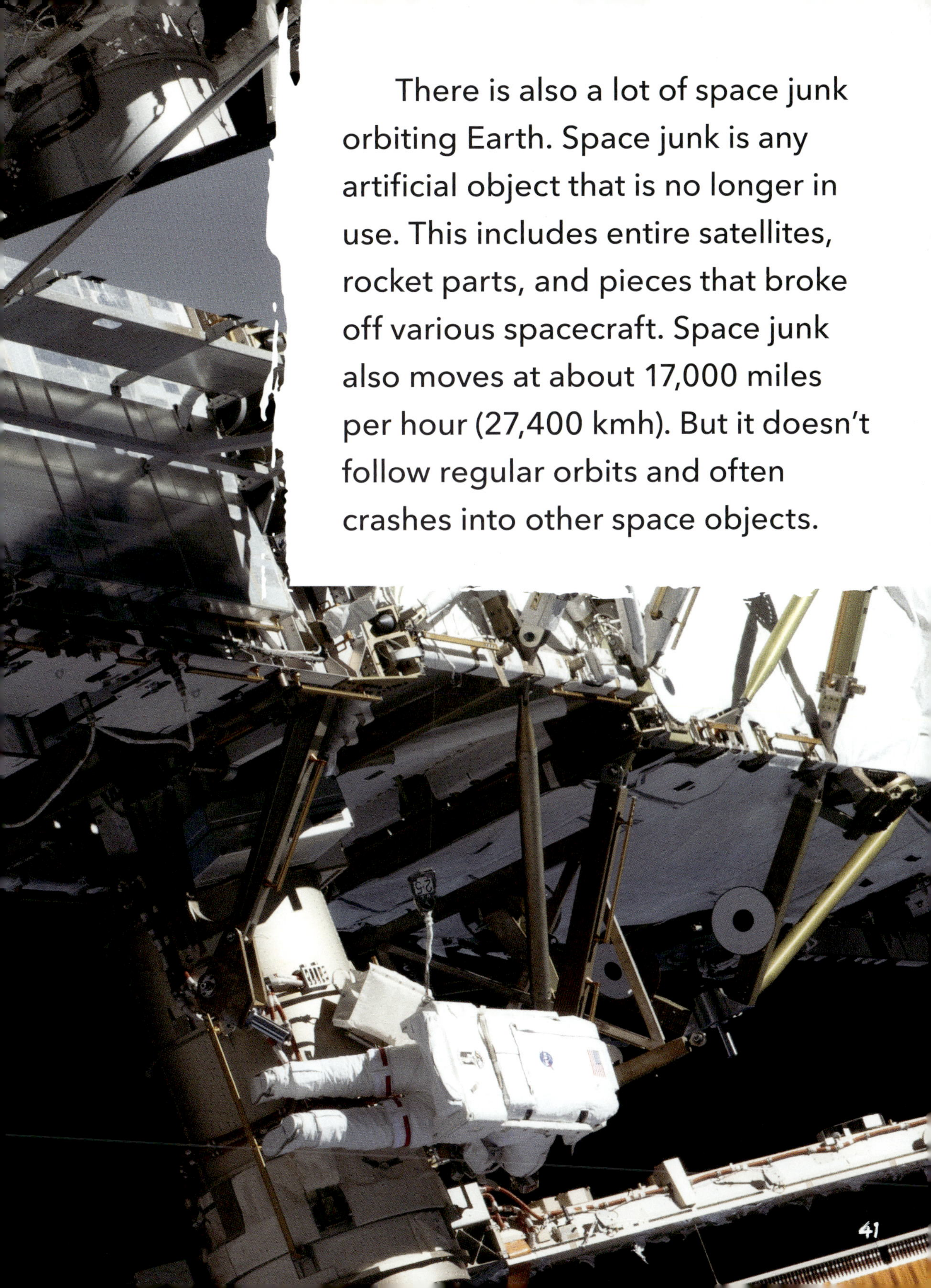

There is also a lot of space junk orbiting Earth. Space junk is any artificial object that is no longer in use. This includes entire satellites, rocket parts, and pieces that broke off various spacecraft. Space junk also moves at about 17,000 miles per hour (27,400 kmh). But it doesn't follow regular orbits and often crashes into other space objects.

NASA launched the Parker Solar Probe in 2018.

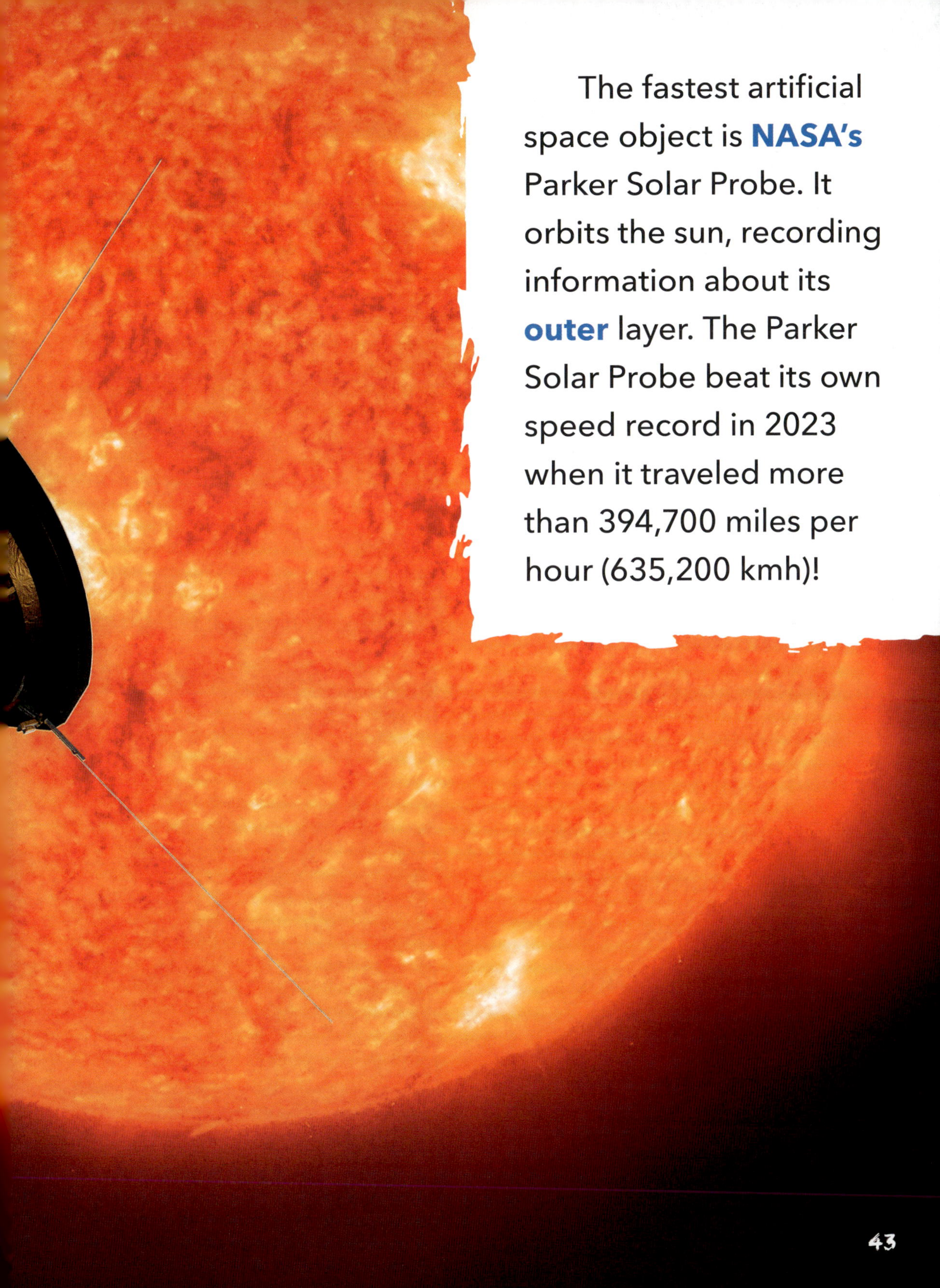

The fastest artificial space object is **NASA's** Parker Solar Probe. It orbits the sun, recording information about its **outer** layer. The Parker Solar Probe beat its own speed record in 2023 when it traveled more than 394,700 miles per hour (635,200 kmh)!

CHAPTER 10

SPEEDING THROUGH SPACE

The fastest things in the universe include natural space objects such as comets, asteroids, and meteoroids. They also include artificial space objects such as satellites and space junk.

Scientists continue to study natural space objects for clues about how the universe and solar system formed. They also work to prevent space objects from crashing into Earth.

Comet NEOWISE

XTREME CHALLENGE

TAKE THE QUIZ BELOW AND PUT WHAT YOU'VE LEARNED TO THE TEST!

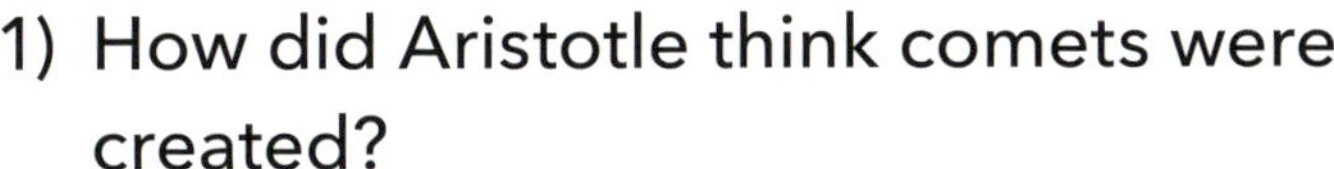

1) How did Aristotle think comets were created?

2) Who discovered that comets travel in regular orbits around the sun?

3) What is the difference between a meteoroid, a meteor, and a meteorite?

4) Have you ever seen a comet or meteor?

5) Can you think of a way to keep an asteroid from hitting Earth?

GLOSSARY

billion—the number 1,000,000,000, or one thousand million.

collision—a forceful crashing together of two objects.

describe—to tell about something with words or pictures.

disaster—a sudden event that causes destruction and suffering or loss of life.

expert—a person very knowledgeable about a certain subject.

launch—to send a spacecraft into space.

light pollution—bright light that comes from artificial outdoor light at night.

NASA—National Aeronautics and Space Administration. NASA is a US government agency that manages the nation's space program and conducts flight research.

omen—something that is believed to be a sign of a future event.

outer—located away from a center or inside.

particle—a very small piece of matter, such as an atom or molecule.

plasma—a type of matter that is similar to a gas but that can carry electricity.

predict—to guess something ahead of time on the basis of observation, experience, or reasoning.

streak—a long, thin mark or stripe.

ONLINE RESOURCES

To learn more about comets, please visit **abdobooklinks.com** or scan this QR code. These links are routinely monitored and updated to provide the most current information available.

INDEX